Teaching Dogs to make Better Decisions

Author: Diane L. Bauman
Illustrator: Caitlin Walker

Front cover design and photo:
Bohm Marrazzo Studios,
Boonton, New Jersey

Cover photo: copyright © 2024
LD Bohm Studios Inc.

No part of this book may be used or reproduced in any manner without the written permission from the author.

First edition. All rights reserved.

copyright © 2024 Diane L. Bauman
ISBN: 978-1-959700-46-3
Hoot Books Publishing
Owner, Victoria Fletcher
851 French Moore Blvd.
Suite 136 Box 14
Abingdon, VA 24210

Table of Contents

ACKNOWLEDGMENTS 5
DEDICATION 6
ABOUT THE AUTHOR 7
FOREWORD 8
INTRODUCTION 10

SECTION ONE

1. WORDS 15
2. SPEAKING DOG 23
3. HOW DOGS THINK 30
4. DOGS ARE SITUATIONAL 37
5. HOW DOGS LEARN 40
6. UNDERSTANDING PUPPYHOOD 48
7. FEAR OF FAILURE 55
8. RELEASE COMMAND 57
9. CONSISTENCY 59
10. TRIAL AND ERROR................................62
11. DISTRACTION..66
12. PROOFING..................................... 68
13. THE POWER OF TIME 71
14. DIFFERENT BREEDS OF DOGS................73

SECTION TWO

15. MANIPULATE THE DOG'S WORLD..............77
16. MOUTHING/PUPPY BITING........................80
17. HOUSEBREAKING....................................82
18. STEALING OFF THE COUNTER.................90
19. BARKING...92
20. PULLING ON THE LEASH..........................94
21. DIGGING..97
22. HOUSEHOLD DESTRUCTION....................99
23. COMING WHEN CALLED.........................102
24. TEACHING STAY....................................110
25. WORKING WITH SHY DOGS....................113
26. UNDERSTANDING RESOURCE GUARDING.117
27. INTRODUCING NEW DOGS.....................121
28. DOGS ARE MY TEACHERS.....................125

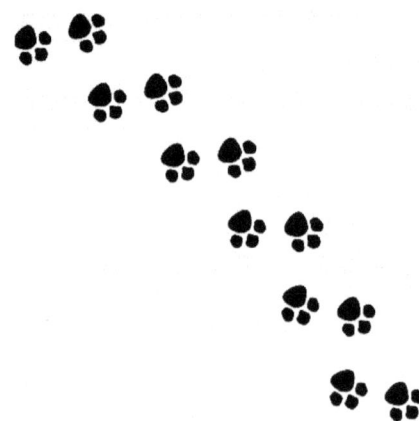

ACKNOWLEDGMENTS

For over 50 years I have worked and lived with anywhere from 2 to13 dogs in my home. From the day I picked up a leash to communicate with dogs, I have never stopped searching for the best ways to reach the soul of dogs. Every dog I have spent time with has taught me things. I want to thank the thousands of dogs who were patient and honest with me as I learned their language. After many years, I have become fluent in the language of dogs and set out to teach it to others.

I also want to thank my students for asking such good questions and for presenting me with challenging problems to solve. It is because of them that I have continued to grow as a canine communicator.

This book is the culmination of what I have learned over five decades. A special thank you to all my friends, relatives and students who graciously offered to proofread this book. Thank you for making this project a reality.

DEDICATION

This book is dedicated to all the misunderstood dogs, including those living in shelters and foster homes waiting for one person to reach out and offer them a future.

ABOUT THE AUTHOR

Diane Bauman is an internationally known obedience and agility instructor and has given clinics all over the United States and Canada. She is the author of Beyond Basic Dog Training (Howell/ Wiley) third edition which has been in print since 1986. Diane has other books and videos (obedience and agility) available on her website:
www.dianebauman.com

The author's record includes 16 perfect scores of 200 in AKC Obedience competitions earned on four different breeds of dogs as well as being a member of the prestigious AKC World Agility Team in 1998, 1999, and 2000 winning gold and silver medals. These accomplishments are proof that the methodology and techniques Diane employs are effective with multiple breeds and withstand the stress of distractions in the real world.

Many of Diane's stars have been dogs rescued from shelters. Currently she resides in East Tennessee on a 32-acre farm where she still trains dogs, teaches both competitive students and pet owners, and rehabs shelter dogs, many of which were considered untrainable.

FOREWORD

I first met Diane Bauman in 1983, and she forever changed the way I approach dog training. Diane taught me that dogs have the ability to "solve problems" and that most mistakes they make are due to confusion rather than deliberate disobedience. She showed me that there are countless ways to communicate with dogs when they don't understand what we're trying to teach them.

While animal behavior is a science with much to offer, nothing compares to Diane's decades of hands-on experience with thousands of dogs and their owners. She has coached owners with dogs of every age, size, and breed, shared her home with an impressive variety of dogs, and participated in countless dog sports. This wealth of experience has given Diane a perspective few of us will ever achieve.

Diane has dedicated her life to observing, listening to, and learning from every dog whose leash she has held. She has continuously expanded her knowledge and deepened her understanding of what drives canine behavior and reactions.

I have been blessed to spend my life training dogs, and I owe much of that to Diane, who sparked my curiosity about the best ways to communicate with them.

If you share your life with a dog and want to improve your dog's ability to make better decisions, Diane can make the journey easier than you ever imagined.

Connie Cleveland-Nolan
www.ObedienceRoad.com
2024

INTRODUCTION

I used to dream of having a magic wand. I would tap my dog on the head and for five minutes, he would understand all of my words. I thought about what the most important things would be that I would want to tell him. "I love you!" "You can't potty in the house, just go outside." "When I call you, drop what you are doing and come to me." "NO means stop what you are doing no matter how much you want to do it!" I could solve so many problems if I just had 5 minutes of conversation with my dog and he would actually understand. But alas, dogs don't comprehend our verbal language and there is no magic wand.

We love our dogs and want nothing more than to talk to them. Dogs were bred for hundreds of years to work with humans (i.e. herding, hunting, protection) and to seek a relationship with two-way interaction. The purpose of this book is to teach you the language and nature of dogs so you can connect and communicate with them easily.

The biggest hurdles dog owners face is understanding how dogs think, how they learn, why they do what they do, what they understand, and what they are trying to tell us. As a dog trainer for over fifty years, the most common complaint I have heard from owners is, "My dog doesn't listen!" This always makes me think of a person standing in a distant country where they don't understand the language. I guess the people in this country, trying to make conversation in the unknown language, might come to the conclusion this person wasn't listening to them since they couldn't illicit a correct response. They might even conclude the person was stupid or stubborn! Most dogs do begin by listening to the sounds we utter, but when owners repeat strange words that make no sense, over and over, dogs inevitably learn to tune them out.

I have always viewed dog training as teaching dogs to make better decisions. As a species, dogs are very capable of problem-solving, which involves thought. Encouraging dogs to think earns them a sense of accomplishment and promotes creativity and effort. A dog that is not afraid to make a decision or offer a behavior (even if it is incorrect) is a dog that is easily guided into good behavior. Permit your dog *"the right to be wrong"* and he will learn to work *with* you. By encouraging a dog to think and problem solve he learns to trust you as a partner and look to you as a teacher. He is not fearful of corrections or confused, thinking only about where the next treat is coming from. It's important, as you attempt to educate a pup, that you do nothing to stifle initiative. Encourage all effort, praise every correct response no matter how small, and ignore or interrupt unwanted behaviors.

Most people think of dog training in terms of positive praise and treats, or negative correction and punishment. These are two extreme ends of the spectrum. There are trainers who pride themselves on using only praise and treats and others who call themselves "balanced trainers" believing you need both positive and negative techniques to train dogs. Some even choose to use electronic collars to train all commands! What if we could educate dogs without bribery or punishment? What if we are positioned in the middle of the spectrum and learned to instruct dogs in their own, familiar language?

Dogs always do what they believe is to *their advantage* to do. When a dog jumps up on a person and gets a scratch on the head or attention from the person, the dog is more likely to repeat this behavior. If a dog is barking and the owner shouts at the dog to "be quiet," the dog's interpretation is the person is also barking at the distraction and this becomes an empowering thing to do. Since the dog does not understand the verbal "be quiet" instruction, future barking is likely to continue anytime the dog sees or hears something novel. Since the distraction that prompted the barking often leaves, the dog is further rewarded by a sense of power as he believes he scared the noise or object away. Every time a delivery truck comes to the house, the dog's barking behavior is reinforced when the truck drives away. The dog feels a sense of accomplishment and is proud of his actions. He has mastered his job of keeping intruders away from his home.

Dog training is nothing more than getting dogs to choose to do what you want them to and make them think it is their idea. The longer I work with dogs (now 52 years), the more I have come to view "training" as the art of manipulation. When you learn how to create an environment where the dog chooses to offer the behavior you want, you have changed his behavior, or "trained him." Examples of this will be shown in future chapters. To my way of thinking, you have encouraged him to make better decisions!
Attempting to force a dog to do something rarely works. Even if you accomplish the task, the dog will only respond correctly if you are close by to pressure or threaten him. While bribing a dog with a treat seems a little more effective, it too has limitations. When you train your dog with only a treat reward, you are setting up a "let's make a deal" scenario. What you produce is a dog that only performs when he is hungry and a treat is forthcoming. While treats can be useful to teach new behaviors (especially with

puppies), they should never be used as bribery. If a dog assumes he will receive a treat for coming when called, what happens when the dog is out in a field eating a dead carcass? Now the dog is not hungry and sees no reason to perform a recall.

SECTION ONE

CHAPTER 1

WORDS

Remember, the most common complaint I hear from humans is that their dogs don't "listen to them." Actually, this is rarely the case. Dogs have excellent hearing and listen well; they just don't understand.

People are obsessed with words; dogs are not. Dogs have no verbal language. You never see two dogs meet and discuss things. The language of dogs is motion. Tails wag, ears go up and down, lips open and close, hair on their backs stands up or lays flat, bodies stiffen or crouch, etc. In seconds, dogs communicate with other dogs and decide friend or foe, play or work, happy or frightened. When humans attempt to communicate with dogs verbally, by issuing commands or "yammering" a stream of sentences ("Get over here!" "What did I tell you?" etc.), dogs are confused. When voices are elevated, or commands are repeated over and over, dogs become concerned and fearful, and either demonstrate avoidance or learn to ignore the human.

Remember, when people yell at dogs, the dogs interpret it as if the human is barking at them. Their perception is the human is upset and worried, not that instructions are being issued.

Why do people repeat commands and raise their voices? When humans feel they are not being understood, their natural reaction is to repeat and speak louder. Have you ever watched two humans having an argument with each other? Undoubtedly, the volume goes up.

While it is true that dogs can eventually learn to associate some word sounds with behaviors, this takes time, patience, and teaching. Usually, when dogs first learn to respond to words, they are not in an aroused state or moving. A dog on a "Sit-stay" when called to "Come" responds easily. Take this same dog and put him in a situation where he is chasing prey or running with another dog and there is often no response to the verbal command of "Come."

When you do attempt to teach dogs verbal language, the first, most important words you should teach are "good" or "yes" which indicates approval from the human. It is not necessary to touch (stroke or pet) a dog as you verbally praise him. Actually, physically touching the dog as you verbally praise him works to distract the dog's brain. It's like he says, "Oh, that feels so good... now what was I doing that you liked?" This slows down the dog's ability to learn. Imagine getting a massage while trying to add a list of numbers. You might experience what the dog does in response to human stroking.

Once a dog understands what praise ("Good!" "Yes!") sounds like, you have a valuable tool to instruct and encourage a dog to repeat desirable behaviors. Feel free to pet your dog in everyday life but **not** as a reward for good behavior. When attempting to impart knowledge to your dog, keeping your hands off him actually speeds up his learning process!

People waste a lot of time telling dogs what they **don't** want them to do. "No bark, no sniff, don't chew that, do not pull, no jumping…" Saying "NO" to a dog is about as helpful as making a shopping list of everything you *don't* want to buy in the grocery store! How long will it take you to shop? Obviously, it is a lot simpler and much more efficient to carry a list of every item you want to purchase when shopping. There is no reason to clutter your mind with information about products on the shelves you do not wish to buy. Experience has taught me, this same principle applies when we strive to communicate with dogs. Why clutter the dog's mind with things you don't want him to do?

Is it helpful to tell a dog when he has made a mistake? Training dogs of all different breeds and ages has taught me that there is no advantage to verbally informing a dog that he has made a mistake. This information, that an error has occurred, can be imparted by withholding praise and/or rewards, repeating an exercise, standing still and showing no emotion, or by gently repositioning or guiding the dog. The training goal should be to subtly alert the dog that something is not right and encourage him to figure it out and try harder next time. Every dog will learn to realize when he is in error without having to be verbally chastised. This approach works to keep the dog thinking about desirable behaviors and avoids the chance the dog will develop any fear of failure. (More on this later.)

Why do people feel the need to tell dogs when they are wrong. Perhaps it's because humans learn better when given verbal feedback about how they are performing. Remember the game of "Hot -Cold" as a child? Someone picks an object in the room while the other person playing is out of sight. When the hidden person returns, the goal is for he/she to figure out what object was chosen. They are coached with words like "you're getting warmer, now you are only lukewarm, now you are cold, getting warmer again, really getting warm, now you are hot and have found the object!" When we attempt to apply this learning approach to dogs, we forget one important factor. Dogs live in the present. What the dog did seconds ago does not play a role in his learning. Once the dog moves in the incorrect direction, it is in his past. If ignored, he will, through trial and error, eventually move in a preferred direction. If the preferred direction is praised, the movement is more likely to continue. The information about what the dog did that was wrong is not helpful because it causes the dog to *think* about what you *don't want*.

Since dogs don't naturally understand verbal language, when a human expresses verbal disapproval, dogs often overreact. Dogs will tolerate physical interruption (like a mother dog would give) much better than any verbal correction.

I often tell people that if saying "NO" would stop a dog's behavior, we wouldn't need dog trainers! When trying to change behaviors, it is always more efficient to give the dog a list of what he does that you approve of. This is accomplished by praising all desirable behaviors.

If every time your dog stayed quietly at your feet, walked calmly at your side, or was quiet when a truck drove past your house and you verbally praised him, he would have a much better idea of how he should behave in those scenarios. One of the biggest mistakes made by dog owners is *not* verbally praising dogs enough for good behavior. If you take good behavior for granted, it will eventually disappear. In the dog training world, we understand that "unrewarded behavior will extinguish." (More on this later.)

- **STOP TALKING, BRIBING, TOUCHING, and telling him when he is wrong.**

HOW TO ELIMINATE UNWANTED BEHA00VIOR

Sometimes there is no good behavior to praise. What do you do then?

What if a dog is barking at a truck? How can you stop this unwanted behavior without the use of "NO!"? Answer: Interrupt it! You can easily interrupt **any** unwanted behavior with touch or sound. A tug on a buckle or martingale collar with a leash, a sudden touch/tap/poke from your hand, or the sound of shaking pennies or pebbles in a can or bottle, will instantly, albeit momentarily, interrupt what a dog is thinking/doing. If you follow this moment of quiet, immediately with praise, the dog begins to understand what you want.

For example: If you repeatedly interrupt the thought pattern of a dog that is contemplating eating your couch, and then praise him for *not* eating the couch, the dog will find something else to think about. It may not be exactly what you want, but if you continue to interrupt all unwanted behavior, and praise good behaviors, the dog begins to understand and learn what you expect of him. Unrewarded, interrupted behaviors will extinguish themselves!

The basic rule is to interrupt behavior you are trying to extinguish and praise what you choose to encourage.

Timing is very important. From a human perspective, praising so close to the unwanted behavior might seem like you are praising the dog for barking or eating the couch. Remember, dogs live in the present. To them, the instant they stop barking, the praise is for being quiet; not for barking. Many owners cause the dog to be quiet and then verbally say "NO" and lecture the dog about bad barking behavior. While the person is referring to the previous behavior, the dog's brain has already moved on to the next action. To the dog, the "No" response refers to the current state of being quiet which is very confusing.

CHAPTER 2

SPEAKING DOG

I label interacting with a dog through praise and interruption: "Speaking Dog." This is the language the mother dog (bitch) uses on her puppies when they are very young. Mother dogs can often be observed pinning a pup to the ground or nipping with teeth to interrupt bad behavior. No mother dog ever lectures puppies! As a result, dogs grow up tolerating and naturally understanding physical interruption much better than verbal harshness. Once a human learns to "speak dog," explaining things to dogs gets much easier and less frustrating for both. The longer I train dogs, the less I say to them, and the faster they learn.

People generally think in terms of words. We naturally choose to communicate using spoken language. Dogs do not easily relate to words as they have no verbal language of their own. *The language of dogs is motion*. Dogs actually see things move faster than people do. Dogs are hardwired to watch motion which makes them good at hunting and herding. (People find it easier to see stationery objects rather than movement.) If you move simultaneously, as you give a command, a dog will focus on the motion and pay little attention to the verbiage. When people realize this, they are careful not to move, when teaching a verbal command.

If you turn and run, most dogs will chase you; known as prey drive. If you quietly pat your leg, many dogs will come closer. If you raise your hand and arm up high (like you were going to throw a ball away from you) many dogs move from you. If you look away, dogs feel less threatened. If you face a dog head-on, you put pressure on the dog to move away from you. By working with someone who speaks "dog," or experimenting, you too can learn to speak the language of "Dog."

Dogs can eventually learn the voice/sound of a person talking to them. When used, verbal commands should be short, typically one word. When teaching a dog to associate a verbal command (word) with an action, the dog must focus on the command word. For this reason, I never use the dog's name before a command. Dogs listen to the very first thing you say. If you preface every command with their name, they think their name *is* the command. In reality, the only time you need a dog's name is if you have more than one dog and only want to command a specific dog.

To *teach* a verbal command, use only the *command* words ("SIT," "DOWN," "STAY," etc.)

People choose to preface a command with a dog's name because humans feel this gets the dog's attention. The truth is, dogs often pay attention to you without looking at you. (Only people customarily look at you to offer attention.) Never confuse *attention* with a dog's head position. Saying a dog's name may make them turn their head towards you but it does not assure you have captured their focus. Think about the dog that is herding sheep. The dog's head is turned towards the sheep, but he can still pay attention to the handler and listen for commands. The same situation occurs on the agility course (i.e. obstacle course of jumps, tunnels and other equipment for dogs.) The dog is looking ahead for the next obstacle but listens closely and pays attention to where the handler is on the course so that he knows which way to turn.

Once a dog learns a verbal command, if you have a multi-dog household, you can then preface the command with a specific dog's name. So, if you only want "Duke" to come to you and Duke knows what "Come" means, you can say, "Duke, Come." Remember, you didn't teach the command "Come" with the dog's name.

WHAT A DOG UNDERSTANDS

In addition to finding words foreign, dogs do not understand sentence structure, adverbs or negatives in a sentence. If you say to a dog, "Don't lie down," all he hears is ``Lie down." If you comment, "Good Sit" to a dog who is already in a sit position, he becomes confused as he does not comprehend that the "good" refers to the sit. He hears "sit" when he is already doing it. How can you instruct a dog to "sit" which requires action, and then say, "good sit" which requires no action, without creating confusion? Dogs never learn to spell and don't value commas. They respond, after careful teaching, to sounds, which is why they can also be taught to acknowledge whistles.

From a training perspective, owners should never continually talk to their dogs with a stream of verbiage that the dog does not understand. This "yammering" as I call it, encourages a dog to tune out the voice of the owner since it makes no sense. Dogs are not "little people in fur coats" and they enjoy quiet time and physical contact. If you want your dog to *hear* you, stop talking so much!

Learning to communicate with dogs is not difficult but it does require the person attempting to impart knowledge understands how canines see the world. It has been said that dogs never get any smarter than a 2-year-old child. (Google it!) My experience supports this theory. We must not work to complicate information if we are dealing with the cognitive level of a young child. Two-year-olds are smart and can be manipulative, but they are not adults.

There are obviously major differences between children and dogs. A child is aware of time and thinks about the past and the future. For this reason, a "time-out" approach may work to change a child's behavior. A child can comprehend if he is mean to a sibling he might have to spend time in his room. Dogs do not understand the concept of a "time-out." If a dog makes a mistake and you put him in a crate, the dog that lives in the present does not realize he is being confined because of previous behavior. While the crate may work to calm the dog down or avoid an immediate repeat of the unwanted behavior, it does not *teach* the dog that he did something wrong. Interrupting unwanted behavior at the time it occurs, can do that. To the dog, his owner just decided it was time for the dog to go in a crate. (More on this later.)

Dogs are forever trying to understand their environment. They do this by testing. A dog gets onto the kitchen counter to see if there is something he might want to eat. A dog digs to see if a smell will lead to a small animal living beneath the surface. A dog barks to see how it will affect the people and other animals around him. A dog steals something and runs off to see if anyone or anything will chase him. Based on the results of these "tests," the dog will decide whether these behaviors are worth repeating. Before an owner/trainer can get a dog to make better decisions, they must understand a dog's *assumption of approval*. What is this?

When you are with your dog (either on or off leash) and the dog does something (like jump, growl, whine, etc.), if you ignore the behavior, the dog *assumes* you approve of what he is doing. To the naïve dog owner, this can be very dangerous. Take, for example, a person out walking their dog in the neighborhood. As their dog notices another dog across the road walking on a leash, the dog gives a low growl. If the owner ignores or excuses this behavior, the dog learns this is good behavior. The next time this dog sees a dog across the road, the growl is louder and lunging behavior accompanies it. So, without even realizing it, the owner has instructed the dog to growl and act aggressively towards a dog across the street that is non-threatening. This owner has failed the dog's test. If the owner had immediately interrupted the dog's low growl (with a touch) and followed it with praise for being quiet, the dog would learn the behavior it was testing was not appropriate. A few more such tests and the dog understands that dogs on leashes across the street are no threat.

- **SIMPLE, LIMITED WORDS AND LIFE IN THE PRESENT**

CHAPTER 3

HOW DOGS THINK

Anyone who has ever lived with dogs and is observant has watched dogs think. Dogs are, by nature, very good problem solvers. How do I get the human to give me a cookie? How do I get the tennis ball from under the couch? How do I get this door to open? Daily, dogs evaluate their environment and ponder how to get what they want.

Dogs always live in the present. They do not spend time thinking about what happened yesterday or what they might get to do tomorrow. Dogs have no sense of time, which is why if you leave them for a few minutes to put a letter in the mailbox, they greet your return with the same enthusiasm as if you had been gone for hours. If a dog chews something up and the owner attempts to change behavior with a "time out" in a crate, it will not work. Explained earlier, the dog does not associate the act of putting him in a crate as a penalty for what happened even minutes before. The dog's conclusion is the owner decided to confine him. While this may manage the immediate act of chewing, it does not teach the dog what you would like him to chew.

For humans, this is very important information. If a dog does something wrong, and you do not catch him in the act, any discipline you try to impose, **after** the fact, is useless at best and more likely damaging. People may claim that if they point to the chewed couch and exclaim, "What did you do?" that the dog acts ashamed. What they don't realize is that even if something or someone else damaged the couch, when you reprimand the dog, he will respond in the same manner. The dog has learned that a chewed couch and you yelling at him are a bad combination and so he cowers. The problem is, the dog has no idea what happened, who did it, or why. This "after the fact" attempt at discipline does nothing to improve future behavior, but it can cause a dog to fear you or fear failure. Dogs fear what they do not understand. Since dogs learn by trial and error, *a dog afraid to make a mistake is difficult to teach. (*More on this later.)

If a dog runs off and refuses to come when called, the dog has learned it's fun to run free. When the dog eventually makes his way home, if he is disciplined or chastised, he learns **not** to come home. A dog does not have the mental ability to understand the punishment refers to the behavior that occurred long before the dog returned home. It is *never* a good idea to punish a dog that has returned home. Coming home should always be a positive experience.

<u>The only successful way to change/ stop unwanted behavior is to interrupt it *as it is happening* and then follow it immediately with praise, once it has stopped.</u>

If a dog runs off when attached to a long leash/line, the line stops the action, and when the dog returns, he is praised. By interrupting the act of running away, the dog learns it is not to his advantage to run away when being called. (More on teaching recall later.)

Because dogs have no verbal language of their own, they think in terms of pictures. This is similar to how people with autism describe their thoughts. Check out: *Thinking in Pictures, Expanded Edition: My Life with Autism paperback– Illustrated, January 10, 2006* by Temple Grandin (Author), Oliver Sacks (Foreword)

An example of thinking in pictures occurs when teaching a dog to lie down. The dog learns what it looks like (the site picture) when he is lying down. If he gets rewarded for repeating this picture, he eventually learns the meaning of the word "down." The problem humans run into is that because dogs think in pictures, every time you ask for a down position in a new location, to the dog, it is a different task. (More on this when we discuss why dogs are situational.)

This "thinking in pictures" concept plays an interesting role specifically when we attempt to teach a dog to come when called (recall.)

To a human, the important part of teaching recall is the dog moves towards the handler when called. In reality, for the dog, the important part is what picture is created when the dog arrives at the handler. If the dog is instructed to sit in front of the handler or come to one side and sit, then that is the "site picture" the dog associates with the "Come" command. When the dog hears the handler command, "Come," the dog works to create the picture of him in front of or at the side of the handler, which in effect, produces the recall. If a handler does not require a consistent position near him at the completion of the recall, the recall concept is vague and very difficult for the dog to learn. When you work to understand how the dog views things, it's much easier to educate him! How do I know dogs think in pictures? Because every time I teach a dog something and change the environment (the picture), the dog acts as if he never learned it. We call this being "situational" and will discuss it in detail later in the book.

While it is true dogs live in the present, they are capable of remembering sequences of events and are very good at anticipating them. This is why, if you dress a certain way, your dog knows whether you are going to work or are staying home. Dogs spend a lot of time studying their owners. They don't have much else to do! When you pick up the car keys, the dog anticipates he may go for a ride. When you open a certain cabinet, the dog expects a cookie. Dogs are exceptionally good at anticipating, which is one reason why they can be trained. In fact, for a dog, the first step of learning something is anticipation. If you want an indication your dog is learning, watch for the dog to offer the new behavior (anticipate) before you have asked for it!

Part of good dog training is teaching dogs *when* to anticipate, and when to wait for a command or cue before offering a behavior. While the anticipated behavior demonstrates a degree of understanding, we should not encourage unwanted anticipation. If a dog learns that when he puts himself into a sitting position in front of you, he earns a treat, he will eventually sit before being asked, as if he is demanding a reward. Make sure it is the dog that is getting trained, and not you! To discourage anticipation, ignore the behavior and begin again.

Unrewarded behavior will extinguish itself.

Dogs subscribe to the belief that when they are confused, it's a good idea to "look busy." It's very common when teaching a dog a new command, if uncertain, the dog's solution is to sniff the ground, bark, tug on your pants leg, jump at the leash, grab a toy, eat grass, wander, run around, or in general *look busy*. We also see this behavior with young children who avoid responding by opting to "change the channel." How often has a parent instructed a child to "go to bed" only to have the child respond by saying, "I'm thirsty." Changing topics is a diversion technique frequently employed to avoid a behavior either because it is not desirable or not understood. If young children can do it, so can dogs!

Trainers may think a dog with his nose on the ground is distracted. In reality, it is more likely the dog is avoiding the command because he is confused. It's as if the dog says, "When in doubt…. sniff." I always assume sniffing is avoidance until proven otherwise.

DOGS THINK IN PICTURES

CHAPTER 4

DOGS ARE SITUATIONAL

When a dog learns something new, the learning process incorporates the location in which the learning takes place. For example, if you teach your dog to assume a sitting position when he hears the command, "Sit," and you do this in your kitchen, you cannot assume the dog will generalize the concept and understand what "Sit" means if you are outside on the grass. Since humans generalize concepts easily, this often upsets people. How often have I heard, "You know how to 'sit'. You always do this at home!" Sometimes owners interpret the dog's lack of response to be a "stubborn personality." This is far from the truth. The dog has just not been taught under what conditions and where, he must do something.

When we understand that dogs think in terms of pictures, it is easy to see why they are situational.

When I teach one of my dogs something new, I am always shocked and pleasantly surprised if they can demonstrate understanding in a new location. In general, it takes about 35 different site pictures (different places) for the average dog to reach a point where they will generalize a concept to all locations. When we say a dog is particularly smart, what we are really saying is this dog generalizes more quickly than average.

Repetition in familiar places, where the dog already understands, is a waste of your time and the dog's. As soon as a dog performs correctly in one place, you need to move the task to a new location. Once the dog will perform under many different conditions, only then does he generalize and comprehend the task. Good trainers do not waste time asking a dog to perform what he can already do, in the location where he can do it. If a dog figures out how to raid your kitchen garbage, he does not need to repeat it many times so as not to forget. Once a dog truly learns something, he knows it forever! Of course, there is no guarantee that the dog will understand how to raid the garbage in the bathroom, because *dogs are situational*!

Why do people like to give commands to dogs in familiar locations where they will probably respond correctly? Perhaps it is because people like to see their dogs be right! Unfortunately, this is not teaching the dog something new, it's more akin to "putting him through his paces."

CHAPTER 5

HOW DOGS LEARN

How exactly does a dog learn to get into the kitchen garbage? He probably smells something enticing and wants to get to it. This is called motivation. Wanting to get what is in the garbage, the dog interacts with the garbage can; maybe he paws at it, jumps on it, or even tips it over. Through trial and error, the dog figures out how to get what he smells. The smelly thing he eats from the can becomes his reward for tipping over the garbage. Does the dog need to repeat this behavior over and over again in the kitchen to learn it? Or, the next time the garbage harbors a good smell, has the dog already learned how to get into it? If dogs can learn something, like how to tip over a garbage can, so quickly, why do people feel they need to ask dogs to repeat behaviors over and over again in the same location to get them to learn?

Dogs *remember best what they discover (*like how to get something out of a garbage can.*)* With this in mind, I do everything within my power to set up situations where dogs will discover what I want them to learn! Specifics on how to do this will be discussed in SECTION TWO of this book.

All dogs learn by trial and error, and they always do what it is to *their* advantage to do. While it is true that we breed dogs to work for man, it's only when the dog sees an advantage to doing what man wants, that he performs reliably. Keep in mind that if you agree that dogs learn by *trial and error*, you must be willing to allow for error. (More on this later.)

Dogs will work for things they want; just like the dog that worked to empty the kitchen garbage can. Frequently, they work for food, toys, and/or verbal praise from the owner. Some dogs will work for the joy of herding, the challenge of tracking, and the pleasure of running and exercising. Other dogs crave attention from their humans, and they will work simply to interact with people and feel like the center of attention. Good trainers use multiple techniques to motivate dogs to work and never rely on only one.

If a trainer uses only treats to motivate, and the dog is not hungry or the task does not allow for treats, it is not useful. I often think of the dog that has been trained to "come" only to get a treat. What happens when this dog is out in a field and finds a dead animal to eat? When the owner calls the dog, does the dog value the promised treat more than the dead animal? If you are competing in obedience and agility competitions, treats are not permitted in the ring. A dog trained to perform for a treat soon figures out there is no paycheck forthcoming and behaviors wane. What about a Guide Dog or Service Dog that must be trained to ignore food on the ground? How well will training only with treats work for this dog?

While treat training is an integral part of teaching a dog/puppy a *new* behavior, treats should never be used as a bribe or be the sole motivation for performance. Remember, we are teaching dogs to make better decisions, not playing "Let's Make A Deal!"

After initially teaching a behavior using treats, every dog must learn to perform the behavior because the owner/trainer cued him to and not because he is working to earn a cookie. To accomplish this, start with random reinforcement. Use a treat reward occasionally but not for every correct response. Sometimes use an "air-cookie" which is a pretend, (invisible) treat in your hand. At any time the dog does not respond correctly, gently insist on the behavior. Do NOT repeat the command. Do NOT offer a treat.

When you tell a dog that understands how to sit when rewarded with a cookie, he must sit without receiving a treat, the dog may not comply. He is not being disobedient; he just does not understand a "sit" command minus the treat. He is being presented with a new picture. To help the dog learn to respond without the treat, use a collar and leash to gently guide the dog into the correct position and then verbally praise him. Once the dog realizes you "say what you mean and mean what you say" and are willing to help the dog respond to your commands, the dog will begin to understand and perform without being paid. Dogs choose the path of least resistance. The dog learns it is easier for him to do what you tell him to, than to have you help him do it. It's not about needing to correct or punish a dog, but rather teaching dogs to make better decisions. Good decisions are based on making the dog's life easier. *It must be easier for dogs to obey than to defy*. When the dog decides it is easier for him to put himself into a sitting position than to have you do it, he commits to the task (without a treat.)

Imagine you place a dog in a sit and tell him to stay as you walk a few feet away. In the beginning, the dog gets up immediately. You gently reposition the dog and praise him. (Do not repeat Sit or Stay.) If the dog gets up 15 times, you put him back 15 times and each time praise him upon getting into the sit. (Very few dogs will get up this many times in a row.) The dog will soon realize it is easier for him to remain sitting until released than to have to keep getting up and being put back. In other words, the dog will *decide* to remain in the sitting position until he earns the freedom of being released, thus learning to "Stay."

I never use treats to teach a "Stay" command. The reward for staying is that the dog earns a release and can go on with his life. A dog that is thinking about where the cookie is coming from is more likely to move and it takes longer to teach the concept of remaining in place. In general, treats (food) motivate dogs to move. We often use food to motivate a dog to move into a position. Motion is not helpful when teaching the concept of stay. Reward your dog with the freedom to move, praise verbally, and he will learn the value of staying.

As you add new information to old information, you stir up the old information. For example, you teach a dog to assume a sitting position on the command, "Sit." For weeks he is very reliable, and you believe he understands the meaning of the verbal word "Sit." Next, you teach him to assume a down position. As the dog begins to understand and respond correctly to the "Down" command, there will be times when you command, "Down" and the dog will sit. Learning the new "Down" command has now confused the dog in terms of when to sit. In time, the dog will sort out the difference (especially if the tone of voice you use for the "sit" is very different from the tone used for "down.") To minimize this confusion, *always teach the dog to lie down from a standing position, never from a sitting position.* As your dog learns more words, there will continue to be confusion with the original commands you thought he understood. This is a normal learning process for the dog, and we expect it to happen.

When dogs learn new things, they often slow down. No person learns to touch-type at 60 words per minute. We begin slowly and as the links are made in our brains, our speed naturally gets faster. It's the same for dogs. When you are first teaching a dog something new, *you* need to slow down and give the dog time to process the information. Do not expect an immediate response.

Certain breeds of dogs, in particular Hounds (like Beagles, Afghan Hounds, and Bloodhounds) and Terriers (which include Scotties, Kerry Blue Terriers, Border Terriers, Westies etc.) tend to have a longer processing time when learning new things. Issue a new command and then give the dog at least 5-10 seconds to respond before helping the dog to comply. If you move too quickly to use food, your hands, or a collar and leash to create the correct response, you run the risk of having the dog give up and just let you do the work. Thinking takes time. If the dog is not planning to respond because he doesn't understand, giving him time to process will not hurt or help. It will teach the dog you are patient and are willing to wait for him to think. Pushing for a quick response will always backfire and interfere with learning. When a dog does respond quickly to a command, it tells us he has built the pathways in his brain and understands what you instructed him to do.

In any training session, dogs seem to remember best what you teach first and last. Use this to your advantage when planning your lessons. If you are teaching the dog a new concept or working on something the dog has difficulty understanding, begin and/or end a training session with this task.

When teaching dogs new things, it's important you not pet or touch the dog in any way when he performs correctly. While this might sound odd, remember we use touch to interrupt thought. When the dog has a good thought, don't interrupt it with touch! I'm not suggesting you cannot pet or touch your dog in everyday life, just refrain from petting for praise when teaching. Keep all praise VERBAL and allow the dog to think about the good things you want him to learn and remember. If someone touches you on the arm, your brain immediately focuses on the touch, and you are not concentrating on what you just heard or learned. The same is true for dogs.

CHAPTER 6

UNDERSTANDING PUPPYHOOD

While it is true dogs can learn at any age (even "old dogs"), we must remember, along with humans, what they learn first they remember best. In other words, "old habits die hard."

This is why it is important puppies are guided into learning good behaviors before they accidentally (trial and error) learn to do bad things!

If a puppy was born in the wild, he would probably be born in a cave or den with his mother attending to his needs. Instinctively, the puppy would not venture very far away from the den at first. At about 4 months of age, puppies develop independence and begin to wander. This is a natural progression of a puppy growing up.

Let's look at a scenario where a family gets a puppy at about 8 weeks of age. The puppy is not on a leash but appears to "hang around" the family. The puppy might even respond to being called by his name to come. (Using the "come" command would be better!) The people who own the puppy believe the puppy understands the word "come" and assume he will not run away. Unfortunately, this is not true. The puppy stays close to home because he is not confident or old enough to venture out into the big world. Then, just like magic, the puppy becomes four months of age and now he no longer responds to "come" or chooses to stay close to home and the family. If a puppy is not taught to come when called with the use of a long leash as he goes from 3 months to 8 months of age, he will learn how and when he can run away. This does not usually end well. (See SECTION TWO for learning to teach a recall.)

All puppies chew. They explore everything with their mouths because they don't have hands. Puppy teeth are very sharp but will fall out and be replaced with adult teeth during the 4 to 6 month growth period. You cannot stop a puppy from chewing, but you can provide appropriate things for him to chew on so he learns to chew hard marrow bones and non-destructive toys, rather than you, your furniture, or clothing. If a puppy is confined in a crate or a pen with proper chewing objects (hard bones, indestructible toys, etc.) he will get in the habit of chewing good things. If you allow a puppy the freedom to explore your house unsupervised, he will learn to chew dangerous things like electric cords and stuffed pillows. Young puppies are like toddlers. For their safety and education, they need to be limited to safe spaces. With young children, we use cribs and playpens; with puppies we use x-pens and crates.

All puppies and dogs need to learn how to walk on a leash. This requires the pup to pay attention to his person and not pull on the leash. You never know when you will need to travel with your dog or take him to a veterinarian. Good leash manners make this not only possible but enjoyable. My choice of dog collar is a well-fitted, wide, "Martingale" collar. This is a collar that will tighten if the dog pulls back but will not choke the dog. The wider the collar, the less chance there is that the dog can damage his trachea if he feels a tug or pulls on the collar. The Martingale collar removes the danger of a dog backing out of a collar without the risk of choking the dog.

Many people attempt to walk dogs on harnesses. Harnesses *teach* dogs to pull on a leash. This is why we put tracking dogs, guide dogs, and sled dogs in harnesses. We want these dogs to learn to pull! If you don't want your dog to pull you while walking, do not adorn him with a harness! While there are harnesses that supposedly discourage pulling, I have not found them to be effective on most dogs.

When you want your dog to learn to walk on a loose leash, train it with a correct collar and never allow the leash to get tight. *Dogs don't pull; people do!* A dog cannot pull against a leash that someone doesn't pull back. It is natural for most humans, when they feel even slight tension on a leash, to pull back. This creates a "tug of war." If, when the dog tries to pull, the person moves their hand holding the leash, *towards* the dog (instead of hanging on) and then jerks it gently back towards themselves, thus returning it to a loose position, the dog is unable to pull. The instant the leash is again loose, **praise** the dog. The dog will soon decide it is to his advantage to keep the leash loose. (More on this in SECTION TWO.)

WHEN DO PUPPIES START TO LEARN?

From the moment a puppy comes into the world, learning begins. Perhaps the first thing a newborn pup learns is how to fill its belly with milk by sucking on the mother's nipple. Finding the nipple is the first "problem" the puppy must solve. Puppies continue to learn every day of their lives. When their ears open, they begin to understand which sounds represent good things and when noise should be feared. A growl (sound) from the mother or realizing that your mother has her mouth preventing you from moving (touch) is the first interruption a puppy encounters.

Puppies are always learning. It is up to the human to decide *what* the puppy learns. If every time a pup whines in a crate, a person opens the crate and cuddles the puppy, the message is that making noise when you don't like something is a solution to your problem. On the other hand, if every time a puppy whimpers in the crate, the dog is whisked outside and offered a potty break, the puppy learns that making noise will instruct a human to take you outside. Even very young puppies are smart. They quickly realize even if they don't need a potty break, if they want to get out of the crate, they should make noise. The human must be smarter than the dog. If the puppy has recently relieved itself, perhaps interrupting the noise (by tapping the crate) followed by praise for the silence, would be a better choice!

LATENT LEARNING

Sometimes you work with a dog to teach a new concept, and it feels like the dog isn't getting it. Each time you follow through, guide, or help the dog perform the behavior. Regardless of your effort, the dog still doesn't appear to understand. The dog offers few, if any, correct responses. The next day you have no time to train, so there is no lesson. After a few days, you return to training, and all of a sudden, the dog appears to have learned what you were trying to teach a few days ago. How is this possible?

We call this *latent learning*. Most dogs do *not* learn at the moment you are teaching. The information is absorbed, not during class, but rather, as they sleep. I'm sure you have heard the phrase, "Let me sleep on it." This is true for dogs as well as people. I often refer to this phenomenon as "planting a seed." I introduce a new concept briefly, thus planting a seed, and then take a few days off to "let it grow!" This approach works particularly well with sensitive dogs inclined to stress every time they are exposed to something new. By the way, any learning is stressful, and some stress is necessary in life.

CHAPTER 7

FEAR OF FAILURE

Dogs are much more sensitive and intelligent than many humans realize. Like people, some of them suffer from a "fear of failure." When taught understanding (and not patterned), dogs always know when they have made a mistake. They don't need people to point it out. (saying "No!")

Some children are so afraid of making a mistake they become ill at the thought of being tested. I have also encountered many dogs, so afraid of making mistakes, they are demotivated ("shutdown") and find learning very difficult. Some of these dogs were born genetically sensitive and others are the product of unfair corrections caused by disciplining a dog for something he didn't understand. *Fear of failure* hinders learning and should be avoided.

One of the first things I teach young canine students is that it is acceptable to be wrong. Wrong is not bad; it's just wrong. Incorrect attempts are never penalized; they are ignored. This encourages dogs to offer behaviors, even if they are wrong, thus increasing the ability to learn through trial and error. Telling a dog "NO" to stop a behavior does not teach good behavior. Too many "No's" and the dog becomes afraid to try, which interferes with trial-and-error learning. I never say "NO" to my dogs. I just interrupt unwanted behavior with touch or sound and then praise.

CHAPTER 8

RELEASE COMMAND

Dogs can be *taught to remember* what they are doing. This allows us to create the duration of a position. Before you can teach a dog to do something for a period of time, you must teach him a release command. Dogs must know when they are released from performing a task. People use words like "Okay," "Break," "All Done," etc. to indicate to the dog the task has been completed and he is off duty. If your dog does not understand a release command, you cannot teach duration ("STAY").

We teach a dog to "sit." Next, we command the dog to "stay." The problem with most dogs is that the stay is very brief and then they pop up out of the sitting position. If you repeat the command "sit," you do not teach the dog to remember what he was doing (remaining in place.) The dog's perception is you are asking for another sit and stay; not fixing the original one.

My response to a broken "Stay" command is to reposition the dog and praise him verbally. (I do not repeat any command.) This encourages the dog to think about what he is doing which earns him praise.

It puts the burden of responsibility on the dog to *remember what he is doing*. It is not the trainer's job to continually remind the dog (by repeating commands) what behavior is required. *Repeat praise; not commands.*

CHAPTER 9

CONSISTENCY

Dogs thrive on being able to predict your behavior. They spend every day studying your actions and know when you are heading for the cabinet that holds the cookies. Dogs like knowing routines because it gives them comfort that they understand their world. We know because it is their nature to anticipate. Dogs understand black and white; always and never. They become easily confused and uncomfortable with inconsistent owners who think in terms of "If I'm not too tired" or "If I have time."

If you decide to train your dog not to relieve himself in your house (housebreak), you must insist that messing in the house is NEVER acceptable. If you put "Pee-pee Pads" down in the house when it's raining because you don't want to take the dog for a walk, you are telling the dog it is acceptable for him to potty in your house. This sends a very mixed message and confuses the dog. You cannot have it both ways.

If you don't want your dog to jump on guests, do not allow your dog to jump on people at all; even you. It may be cute when a baby puppy puts his tiny paws up on your leg but think about whether it will be equally as cute when the puppy weighs 60 pounds and has wet, muddy feet. Dogs do not understand the concept of "sometimes," "maybe," "until you grow up" and "if it's not raining." *It's either always or never.*

Good dog trainers are consistent with their commands, praise, and expectations. If a dog is expected to walk without pulling on a leash, then he is *always* expected to keep the leash loose. A good dog trainer does not change criteria because the dog is overly stimulated or because the trainer doesn't have time to work with the dog. There are no exceptions to these rules.

If you teach your dog to come to you when you say "Come," then you cannot change the command casually and say, "Come on" or "Come-ere." If you teach your dog that "Down" means lying down on the floor, you cannot tell the dog to "Get down" when he jumps on you unless you want him to end up on the ground. *Consistency with all commands is important.*

Whenever you give a command to a dog, you must be prepared to follow through and get the dog to respond correctly. A wise dog trainer never issues a command he is not in a position to enforce. If your dog is out in the yard and you are in a nightgown dressed for bed, do not call the dog to "come" unless you are prepared to go outside in your slippers and get the dog if he does not obey. Perhaps a dog with minimal recall training should only be allowed outside at night with a long line attached to his collar? This way, if he chooses not to come when called, the owner has a way of insisting the task is completed. When a dog realizes everything you command will happen, and you will only say it once (one command), he will become trained. If you are not willing to "*say what you mean and mean what you say,*" stop issuing commands to the dog!

CHAPTER 10

TRIAL AND ERROR

If you accept dogs learn by trial and error, you must, as a teacher, be willing to accept and even encourage errors. Dogs and people learn from what works to solve a problem as well as what doesn't work.

Thomas Edison was once asked, "How did you have the patience to keep going after failing to make a lightbulb light up 10,000 times?" His response was, "I did not fail. I learned 10,000 things that do not make a lightbulb light up!"

"Error-free learning" is an oxymoron.

There are dog trainers who fear that if they allow a dog to make a mistake, he will learn to make the mistake. This is not true, as long as the incorrect response is not rewarded.

Unrewarded and interrupted behavior will extinguish itself.

Take a common scenario where you put a dog in a chain-link pen. The dog wants to escape the pen and searches for a way out. He may bark, but no one comes to let him out. He may try to dig, but someone has buried wire under the ground, and he cannot dig out. He may try to jump and climb up the side of the pen, but it has a wire top on it. The dog has learned several behaviors that do not solve his problem. Eventually, the dog becomes very frustrated and jumps up and hits the latch to the door of the pen just right. The door opens and the dog is free. The dog does not yet understand what worked to earn him his freedom, but he knows it's possible to get out of the pen.

The next day the dog is returned to the pen. He may bark or dig or climb briefly but soon remembers where he was (the site picture) when the pen opened, and he hangs out by the door. Through trial and error, once again, jumping on the latch produces the reward of freedom. By the third day the dog is placed in the pen, he no longer wastes time doing what doesn't work but puts all of his efforts into jumping on the door near the latch. Soon the dog will learn exactly how to open the door to the pen and will be able to free himself immediately. Once the dog learns this, he will know it forever in that pen. Did we need to concern ourselves with allowing the dog to try things that didn't work to earn his freedom? NO! Unrewarded behaviors are simply extinguished.

There was no need to yell "NO" at the dog when he was barking, digging, or climbing for him to realize these behaviors would be unsuccessful. He figured it out all by himself. This is exactly why *I never tell a dog what not to do.* I prefer to let him figure it out. If the dog decides not to do something, it will be his decision and it will last forever.

Dogs learn things very quickly. They learn what works for them and what doesn't bring the desired response. Of course, they also learn unwanted behaviors just as quickly! If a dog jumps up on your bed or couch one time and feels the warmth and comfort of the soft surface, he has learned how to jump on the furniture in that room. This is why, if you don't want your dog on your furniture, you may never permit it to become rewarding.

Because dogs learn things so quickly, it is not necessary to spend a lot of time training them. Good trainers focus on the quality of training, not *quantity.* When we talk about the need for repetition, remember this only refers to repetition in **new places**. Always work to discover what the dog understands and what he doesn't. Teach the dog what he needs to learn, in the places he needs to learn it. There is no advantage to practice what he has mastered in the locations where the dog is already successful. People who do this like to see their dogs do things correctly, but this is not teaching the dog anything new. Train what the dog is weak on, not what he is good at!

When a dog makes a mistake, this is important information that tells the trainer what the dog does not understand. Just because dogs do something correctly a few times, does not mean they understand what or why it is correct. *Behavior often precedes learning*. If you find yourself saying, "You know how to do this, you did it yesterday," you have fallen into the trap of assuming understanding.

If you have been using one approach to teach a dog something and you do not see progress after a few sessions, try a different approach. Do not continue to explain things in a way the dog doesn't understand. When learning to ride horses, my instructor would always tell me to "keep my heels down." This message continued for years and inevitably my heels were in the wrong place. One day, upon returning from a seminar, my instructor explained, "keep your toes up!" That solved the problem.

CHAPTER 11

DISTRACTION

It is normal for all dogs to get distracted. Puppies and adult dogs are naturally very aware of their surroundings. It is part of self-preservation for dogs to pay attention to sounds and sights around them. As we train dogs, we teach them it is to their advantage to pay attention to us (trainers and owners) so we can instruct them. You cannot force a dog to pay attention. You cannot bribe a dog to pay attention. Attention is a state of mind and not a dog's head position. While you may be able to encourage a dog to turn his head towards you, this is no guarantee the dog is thinking about what you want.

To build an attentive dog student, the trainer needs to make sense by "speaking dog." Good teachers are interesting and unpredictable with the use of food and movement, minimize repetition, and *never wait* for a dog that is not paying attention. If you are teaching a dog to come when called (Recall), never hesitate to call the dog until he is paying attention. This actually teaches a dog if he doesn't want to do something, he should appear to be distracted! At precisely the moment the dog finds a good smell or sees another animal, call him to you and be in a position to enforce the command by interrupting (unwanted behavior) with a long line. Owners who wait for dogs to pay attention before issuing commands are teaching their dogs to tune them out! The dog quickly realizes if he does not pay attention, people wait, and no one will ask him to do anything.

The stronger the distraction, the harder the trainer must work to interrupt the unwanted behavior. A dog smelling a flower can easily be interrupted with a gentle tug on a collar. A dog chasing a cat is going to need a stronger sound or touch to interrupt unwanted behavior. A good instructor can advise the type of collar or sounds needed to provide appropriate interruptions for different dogs and in different scenarios. In extreme cases I have even employed the use of air horns when necessary to interrupt intense behaviors.

CHAPTER 12

PROOFING

Proofing is the concept of testing to determine what a dog knows and under what conditions he knows it. It is checking to see if you have taught the dog many different "site pictures." For example, you teach your dog a "Sit-Stay" in your kitchen, does the dog truly understand what is expected of him or is he just staying because he is waiting for you to put his food down? You don't know unless you test (proof) it. What happens to the dog on a "Sit-Stay" if the trainer drops a toy or food? Bends over? Whistles? Changes locations? Each new scenario needs to be tested and taught to the dog. What happens if the dog gets up off the Stay? Simply return him to the correct position and praise him verbally. No additional commands are needed.

Everything you think you have taught a dog needs to be proofed. This is because *behaviors precede learning.* In other words, dogs often do things correctly but may have no idea what or why they are doing it. If a dog accidentally comes to you because you called him, does that mean the dog understands a recall command? Probably not. A "Come" command needs to work under all conditions, not only if the dog has nothing better to do. Have you taught this? Have you taught it in 35 different locations? Owners and trainers get into a lot of trouble assuming dogs understand things they don't. Correcting a confused dog causes a dog to mistrust and fear making mistakes. Don't assume; proof and then, based on the results of the proof, teach!

Proofing needs to happen at all levels of learning. Proof a Sit-stay when standing close to the dog on a leash. Proof it again as you add distance away from the dog. If you teach a task from beginning to end and *then* attempt to "proof" it, you upset the dog. The dog was under the impression he knew what he was doing. Perhaps you have spent four weeks teaching a Sit-Stay and building distance. Now, at full distance, you add a "proof" and the dog makes lots of mistakes. The dog loses his confidence because he thought he understood, only to find out that now, he can't be successful. If you "proof" (test understanding) frequently, as you progress through the learning stages, the dog's knowledge will be solid and confidence will grow.

When you proof a task and the dog fails, do not correct. Don't even tell him he is wrong. Ignore the incorrect response and help the dog. The proof told you the dog didn't really understand, and you need to *help* the dog understand by showing or guiding. Depending on the task, you may help the dog by simplifying the task or lowering the temptation of the proof. This will encourage the dog to work with you to solve the problem.

CHAPTER 13

THE POWER OF TIME

In the relationship between a dog and a human, the human controls the dog's life. The human decides when the dog eats, rests, goes for walks, learns new things, relieves itself, plays, etc. I refer to this as "the power of time." This power is a very strong force in manipulating dogs to do what we want if we understand how to use it. The first step is for the person to realize there is power in controlling a dog's life. Even the strongest-willed dogs can be coerced into making better decisions when they learn their person controls time.

Take, for example, a dog that you are trying to housebreak. If you take the dog/puppy out on a leash and stay outside, interrupting play, until the dog relieves itself, you have taught the dog that he cannot return to the warmth/cool of the house until he potties. If every time you take the puppy out, you wait for the correct behavior, the dog will learn that to get you to take him inside, he must go to the bathroom outside. I have even had dogs that did not need to pee, fake it, to earn the right to return to the house!

If you have a dog that does not choose to lie down in a new place and you calmly continue to show the dog what you want, eventually the dog will comply. Why? Because the dog learns that to go on with his life, he must do what you say. While it might take you 5-20 minutes to get the dog to lie down the first time (without repeating commands,) each time you give the "down" command in the future, response time gets faster. Eventually, the dog responds immediately because he now realizes life as he knows it does not continue until he does what you have instructed. The dog may not remember what you said to him minutes ago, but he understands the body language you are using to encourage a "down" behavior. Since the word was not understood to begin with, remembering it is not important at this time. Repeating commands the dog does not understand, does not explain the task. When a dog learns you are willing to wait him out until he responds correctly, you are making use of your "power of time" to change behavior.

CHAPTER 14

DIFFERENT BREEDS OF DOGS

Dogs were originally bred to work for mankind in different capacities. Some breedings produced dogs with an accentuated ability to hunt or herd. Others were developed for an enhanced natural ability to scent or an innate tendency to protect. Through selective breeding, man created different breeds of dogs for specific purposes. While it can be said that all dogs are still dogs, when getting dogs to make better decisions, it is helpful to understand the genetic tendencies of different breeds.

Herding breeds often react physically before thinking about why they are moving. I call this, "body in motion before brain." When herding, this is a positive trait. When a sheep attempts to leave the flock, a talented herding dog "covers" the animal and brings it back with split-second reaction time and no conscious thought. If the dog first had to consciously notice the sheep was darting off, it might be too late to retrieve it.

When working with herding (Collies, Shelties, Border Collies) and sporting breeds (Labrador Retrievers, Golden Retrievers, Setters, Pointers) of dogs (or mixes), it helps to understand these dogs will often do something long before they have a chance to think or learn what is expected of them. Trainers see correct behaviors and naïvely assume the dog understands a behavior, when in fact, the dog was just doing "what seemed like the thing to do at the time!"

In contrast, Hounds and Terriers are very thoughtful dogs. Their cautious nature is often misunderstood to be a reluctance to respond (sometimes even referred to as stubborn.) These breeds carefully assess the situation before putting their bodies into action. If a Terrier is hunting a mouse/mole, it checks out where the scent is coming from and investigates the environment before starting to dig. When attempting to communicate with a hound, the trainer must allow the dog an extended period of "processing time" (5-15 seconds) before expecting a response. No need to repeat commands, just wait. As Hounds and Terriers learn, their response time naturally increases. If you try to push these dogs to react before they have thought about what you want, they resist and lock up. I equate it to asking your computer to do something and the computer has a circle spinning as it is processing the command. If you continue to bang on the keys, it doesn't get any better and the computer might even freeze up!

Dogs bred for protection are often hyper-alert to their surroundings as they would need to be if protecting something or someone. Not surprisingly, these breeds are very easily distracted by their environment. This must be addressed when training tasks other than what they are specifically designed to do. While you are never going to convince a German Shepherd or Belgian Malinois to ignore his surroundings, you can teach them to multi-task and respond to your commands in addition to being aware of their surroundings.

Sighthounds (Greyhounds, Afghan Hounds, Whippets, etc.) with their superior distance vision present interesting challenges. They often view things differently and are hyper cautious and aware of their environment even at a distance.

As you learn to understand different breeds of dogs, you realize the language of "DOG" has many different dialects.

You will always be more successful if you work *with* your dog and not against his natural dog qualities and abilities. While every dog can learn to heel, sit, come, or perform weave poles, they all perform with unique styles as they are different sizes and shapes of canines. Allowing dogs to do what is natural for them, as long as it meets your training criteria, is easier and more dependable. It's going to take a large dog longer to get into a lie-down position than a small dog. A dog with long legs is going to bend more easily than a long dog with short legs (Corgi, Dachshund, etc.) Train the dog you have at the end of your leash and don't try to force all pups into the same mold.

SECTION TWO

CHAPTER 15

MANIPULATE THE DOG'S WORLD

Now that you understand how a dog thinks, learns, and naturally responds to the world around him, you are better prepared to manipulate the dog's environment so that he learns to make better decisions. You are smarter than the dog and should never need bribery or corrections to change a dog's behavior. If you remember that dogs always do what they perceive is to *their* advantage to do, outsmarting them is actually easy. When you manipulate the dog's world, you never do anything to harm or hurt the dog. All techniques are calm and gentle, designed to encourage dogs to think and *make better decisions*!

JUMPING

A dog jumps up on you. Why? Probably because he wants your attention, comforting touch, or to solicit play. If you like your dog jumping on you and your guests, you don't have to change their behavior. But, if you want to get the dog to decide that jumping is not in his best interest, keep reading!

What if, when the dog's front paws touched you, you took hold of them and didn't give them back right away? Holding the paws gently, you tell the dog what a wonderful dog he is and that you are very happy he has decided to give you his paws, as you continue to hold his front feet. If the dog tries to pull his feet away, HOLD ON! Continue to give the dog verbal sweet talk as you maintain control over his paws. No one is angry, but if the dog puts his front paws up on you, he can't have them back. If the dog attempts to chew his feet free, hold them further apart. When the dog starts to show frustration with his predicament, release his feet and praise him *verbally* for having his feet on the ground. Most dogs will immediately try jumping again because they cannot believe their paws got stuck in your hands. It doesn't take long before your dog will decide you are a very nice person who likes him very much, but he is not going to put his feet on you because you are crazy and don't give them back until you want to! Because dogs are situational, you will need to repeat this in different places and with different people, before the dog generalizes all humans have a "doggie paw fetish" and love to take and control the front paws of friendly dogs. The dog has decided that **he** doesn't want to put his feet on people. Since it is the dog's decision, it will hold up over time.

CHAPTER 16

MOUTHING/PUPPY BITING

All puppies explore the world around them with their mouths. After all, they don't have hands. Words do not easily stop this behavior, but actions will.

When a puppy puts his open mouth on your hand or arm, gently take hold of his bottom jaw, and with your thumb of the same hand, press down gently on his tongue. Tell him what a good boy he is and how much you love him. He now has to deal with your hand in his mouth, pressing down on his tongue. When he tries to pull away, after 5 to 10 seconds, on your terms, let go. Repeat as necessary. Would you put your mouth where your tongue would get stuck? No one is angry. The dog learns you play a very strange game of tongue grabbing and he doesn't choose to play.

With some very responsive puppies that have been raised with a litter of siblings, if you whimper like a dog when the puppy puts his teeth on you, they will stop their behavior giving you the opportunity to immediately praise them!

In puppies up to about four months of age, mouthing is easily discouraged without using words. Biting in older dogs is a different issue and needs a different approach. As a new puppy owner, don't let your pup learn this bad habit.

CHAPTER 17

HOUSEBREAKING

The methods used to train dogs, including housebreaking, have improved greatly over the years as we have learned more about how our dogs think. "Paper Training" and "Rubbing His Nose in It" are antiquated techniques, which we now know can produce confused, insecure dogs that often fear, rather than respect, their owners. There is now a much more efficient, safer, kinder way to housebreak dogs.

Not all animals can be housebroken. It's probably not going to happen with a horse! The reason we *can* teach a dog to go to the bathroom out of the house is that nature has given puppies the instinct to keep their beds clean and not to soil where they eat or sleep. Using this knowledge, we use "Crate Training" to teach a dog to be clean in our house which is now his. (More on Crate Training later.)

Unless you live on the sixth floor of an apartment building, NEVER paper/ piddle-pad train your dog. If you do, you are making the job of housebreaking much more difficult by encouraging the dog to think you want him to soil in the house, specifically on something soft. Remember, dogs think in black and white. Help them understand right from the beginning that outside is the only acceptable place to relieve themselves.

Establish ONE toilet place outside. Take the puppy/dog to this location after eating, drinking, awakening, excitement, or active play. Stand with the puppy and give a command to use the bathroom. ("Go Potty," "Hurry UP" or "Do Your Business" are some favorites.) When the dog "assumes the position," praise them verbally. If your puppy would rather play outside and shows no interest in using the bathroom, take him out on a leash. Stand still and allow the puppy to circle in the appropriate area. Always use the same door to lead to the outdoor potty area. The puppy will eventually stand by this door when asking to go out. All dogs should learn to use the bathroom on a leash in case you need to travel with them. If the dog/puppy does not relieve himself, when you return to the house, he must either be returned to a crate or held by you on leash. He can have **no unsupervised** time in the house in which to have an accident that you don't witness.

Feed your dog/puppy at the same times every day. Feed the same food every day. This will help keep the puppy regular and allow you to anticipate when he will need to use the bathroom. Never "free feed" leaving food out all the time. It is not healthy and makes housebreaking very difficult. The water container should be removed at night when the puppy is crated for bed and if you need to leave him for an extended period of time during the day.

Should an accident occur in the house as you are watching, never let the pup see you clean it up. His mother cleaned up after him and that was acceptable. Don't let him think you are there to do the same. Never "Rub His Nose in It" (unless you want to teach him to eat it!) There is no need to scold or spank a dog to Housebreak. When you catch the pup making a mess in the house, interrupt his behavior by picking him up in the middle of his action and take him outside. Praise the pup when you set him down. If your dog is in the habit of soiling in one particular place in the house, start feeding the pup in this location. Turn his bathroom into a dining room! Instinctively, dogs will not soil where they eat or sleep. The older a dog gets without being housebroken, the harder it is to housebreak it. Start housebreaking as soon as you bring a puppy home or acquire an adult dog.

At night or whenever you are unable to carefully watch a dog/pup you are trying to housebreak, the pup should be confined to a crate they cannot get out of. We call this "Crate Training." The crate needs to be large enough for the dog to stand up, turn around, and lie down. Since their instinct tells them not to soil where they sleep, the puppy learns how to control his elimination.

To teach a dog/puppy that a crate is a comfortable place to be, begin by placing a treat in an open crate. Permit the dog to go into the crate on his own, turn around and come back out. If the dog is cautious about entering a confined space, begin with the treat on the edge of the door. Gradually move the reward further and further into the crate. Only after the dog is willingly going into the crate on his own to get a treat at the back, should you proceed.

Wait for the dog to begin to eat the treat you have thrown to the back of the crate and calmly close the door of the crate. This is the first time the dog has been prevented from exiting on his own. Praise the dog verbally for 5 to 10 seconds while he is in the crate and then open the door and allow him to come out. Gradually extend the amount of time the dog is confined to the crate before letting him out. Never open the door if the dog is whining or barking. By waiting for the dog to settle down and be quiet, even for a brief moment, before opening the crate door, the dog learns that complaining does not make the door open. If the dog continues to cry, tap the top of the crate, thus using sound to interrupt the crying long enough to reward the dog by opening the crate. Crate training is a process like all dog training.

Some older or rescued dogs have an aversion to a crate. When put in a crate, they may scream, panic, and even bite at the sides of the crate. This is usually because they have been crated for extremely long periods of time and they are afraid if they enter confinement, it will be a terrible experience. While these dogs can be retrained to like a crate, it takes longer. Start at the beginning and think of the dog as a young puppy first learning about the crate.

If a dog will absolutely not enter a crate head first, back him into it with a cookie. Close the door briefly and then let him out.

If a puppy/dog cries or acts distressed (after having been in the crate for a while) you *must* let him out and take him immediately to the outside bathroom. At night, place the crate near your bed so you can hear the puppy if he wakes up and asks to go out. If you ignore a dog trying to communicate with you from a crate, you will force him to be dirty and ruin his instinct to keep his bed clean.

Is it cruel to cage a dog? Absolutely *not* if the crate is introduced to the dog correctly and the dog is not left in a crate for extended periods of time. Dogs are den animals. In the wild they would live in a small cave or den. A plastic airline crate provides the dog the same secure, safe place that a cave would offer. Dogs usually seek small, confining places such as corners, under tables, desks etc. for security. Since the dog instinctively will not soil where he sleeps and eats, crate training makes use of the dog's natural instinct to housebreak him in a positive way. Think of a crate as a small puppy crib or playpen. Crating a dog for more than 4 hours at a time is not a good situation. While puppies do sleep a good many hours a day, they frequently wake up and need to potty. Depending on the age of the puppy, you might need to employ someone to let your dog out of the crate every few hours when he is young. Some small breed dogs have very small bladders and can need to relieve themselves every 45 minutes when under 4 months of age. Housebreaking takes effort and time and will not happen if you are away at work and your puppy is left alone at home.

If you must work, you will need someone to come and let the puppy out of his crate every 3-4 hours during the day or you might want to consider Puppy Day Care.

Crates can be purchased from airlines as they are used to ship dogs. They are also available in pet stores and online. It's not uncommon to find used crates for a few dollars for sale at flea markets, garage sales, and at online marketplaces.

After you have used a crate to housebreak a dog, it is still valuable. It protects your house from biting teeth and keeps puppies from eating poisonous products and from being electrocuted by chewing on electric cords. A crate provides a safe and convenient seatbelt for your dog in the car. Many dogs that get car sick are better in the security of a crate in the car. If your dog gets sick or undergoes surgery, your vet will instruct you to keep him quiet. With the use of a crate, this is a simple task. When traveling, a crate in a motel room assures your dog will do no damage or stress if you are absent. A dog in a crate cannot accidentally escape out of a room or car. If you are having a lot of company and don't want the dog underfoot or near young children, a crate is a safe place to put a dog. Locking a dog in a room where he can scratch at the door or tying him outside where he might cry or be exposed to the elements is not a good idea.

Puppies purchased in pet stores or kept in dirty cages at an early age are more difficult to housebreak. They have been forced to live in filth where they eat and sleep and as a result, their instinct to be clean is diminished. These dogs need a little extra help as the crate/confinement method does not always work for them. While they should still sleep and eat in the crate during the day, if you cannot watch them, tie them with the leash to your waist. This way, if they start to have an accident you are in a position to interrupt it.

When you can avoid all accidents for three weeks, you are on the way to having a dog that will keep your house clean.

CHAPTER 18

STEALING OFF THE COUNTER

Dogs learn to steal food off a counter by trial and error. Something smells good so they get up on their hind legs and jump to reach the tasty morsel. They are rewarded by eating the stolen food and so the behavior continues. If you yell "no" at the dog or "get off" and push him to the floor, the dog learns as long as you are present to control the thievery, it probably will not work. Dogs are smart. As soon as you depart the room, the counter again becomes fair game.

Never get angry... get even! Plant a tempting treat on the counter. Arm yourself with a soda can with pennies in it or a water bottle with pebbles in it. Maybe even a few items you can hurl through the air across the room. Leave the room and wait. When the dog attempts to steal, throw the object at the counter. If the dog is startled and gets off, run in and rush to his rescue. "You poor baby! Did God throw something at you for getting on the counter?" Once is never convincing, so set it up again. Be sneaky. Try a few hours later when the dog may have forgotten about what happened. Sometimes it takes a few repetitions before the dog decides this crime doesn't pay off as expected! When paws on counters cause things to fly through the air, dogs decide to stay away from them.

CHAPTER 19

BARKING

Dogs bark for many different reasons. People generally want their dogs to give an alert when someone is approaching the house or if there is smoke from a fire nearby. The problem with barking is it's difficult to explain to a dog what is helpful barking and when barking becomes a nuisance. Dogs barking because they are accidentally locked in a room is a good thing. Dogs barking for attention because they don't like being away from their owners is annoying.

As with all unwanted behaviors, we need to interrupt. Arm yourself with things to throw. A heavy piece of chain tied in a small circle (like a bracelet) works well. Empty soda cans with pennies in them will also work. If your dog barks to alert you to a stranger, delivery, or unwanted animal approaching the house, verbally praise the dog and then say, "Enough." Any bark after that will cause an interrupting noise maker to fly through the air. As soon as the noise lands near the dog and the dog quiets (even for a brief moment), praise verbally. You may need to throw more than one thing to get the dog to make a better decision. For sensitive dogs, you might only need to shake the can and the noise will be enough to interrupt the barking.

Since consistency is the key to good dog training, you must be prepared to interrupt unwanted barking *every time* it occurs; not only when you become frustrated by annoying barking. I was once receiving a package from FedEx in my driveway. Seven barking dogs charged the fence. I simply said "enough" one time, and all was quiet. I will never forget the look on the driver's face when he turned to me and asked, "How do you do that?" Truth be told, the dogs knew that following the word "enough," I would take a metal dustpan and scrape it across the chain link fence they stood behind! They all decided being quiet was in their best interest!

Different breeds of dogs are more inclined to use their voices. Some of the more vocal breeds are Papillons, Icelandic Sheepdogs, and Australian Shepherds. Hounds like to howl and many small breeds like to yip in a high pitched repetitive manner. If you own a dog that is genetically inclined to bark, controlling it will take more discipline on your part. Never yell at a dog that is barking. The dog thinks you are barking too!

CHAPTER 20

PULLING ON THE LEASH

Every dog and puppy needs to learn not to pull when on a collar and leash. (Harnesses actually teach dogs to pull which is why we put sled dogs and guide dogs in a harness to encourage them to pull.) How can you tell if a leash is loose? The snap that attaches to the dog's collar should hang down. The dog only understands black and white, all or nothing. You cannot accept even a slight pull, as it will always get worse. Either the dog feels no tension at all on the leash or it is considered pulling. Always use a safe collar (wide Martingale) that will not choke the dog or damage the trachea.

A dog should learn no matter how long the leash is, never pull against it. Start with a six-foot leash (flat and wide works best.) If you feel any tension from the dog, move your hands holding the leash *towards* the dog to make it loose. Next, snap it quickly towards you and then immediately move it back towards the dog to loosen it. A snap is quick but not hard. Think of snapping a rubber band on your wrist. As soon as the leash is loose following the snap, praise the dog. A dog cannot pull against a leash that doesn't get tight. If you never pull back, the dog can't pull. Actually, dogs don't pull; people do!

Most humans naturally react to a pulling dog by *pulling back* to hold on in an attempt to control the dog. This is exactly the opposite of what works. You need to learn to change your natural reaction to get results.

If you are not very strong or are working with a large, heavy dog you might need to employ a slightly different technique. If you sense the leash starting to tighten, move the leash with both hands towards the dog to loosen it and then immediately change direction moving away briskly. The dog will not only feel a quick jerk but will notice you are going in another direction. Praise the dog as soon as he starts to come in the new direction and the leash is loose. Change directions as often as needed.

If a strong dog has been pulling against a leash for a long time, you might need a different collar and/or heavier leash. The wider (not longer) the leash between you and the dog, the faster the dog feels the jerk as the leash does not stretch. A leather or web leash ¾ to 1 inch wide can be very useful with a large dog. Do not attempt to communicate with a large dog using a skinny leash. It's a little like trying to cut a lawn with scissors! If you feel you need a different type of collar to make an impression on the dog, consult a dog trainer who can find the appropriate collar and make sure it is fitted and used correctly. If your technique is not correct, no collar will work. Never use choke collars. You never need to choke a dog to teach him something. When a dog feels like he cannot breathe, he is not in a state of mind where he can learn. Find another alternative!

CHAPTER 21

DIGGING

Dogs are born knowing how to dig. Nature probably gave them this ability so they could bury bones and food for the future. Some dogs still bury favorite items, others dig for fun, as part of hunting moles, etc. Dogs dig to escape a pen or simply because they are bored. Most excavation occurs when dogs are left unattended outdoors for long periods of time. They find digging entertaining and sometimes as a way to find a cool place to lie. The issue with stopping a dog from digging is that while you can stop the activity in one location, the dog will likely move to another spot.

Always provide a dog left outside with plenty of shade and water. Train and exercise the dog before leaving for extended periods of time. Fill bones (raw, large, femur beef bones with marrow removed) with his meals (soaked kibble and frozen) and hide them around the yard.

If you are gone for more than 4 hours, have someone visit and check on your dog. The younger the dog, the more active he will be and the more mental stimulation he will need. Older dogs are more content to sleep for many hours during the day. If you work all day, a puppy may not be suitable for your lifestyle. They do not raise themselves. If you insist on getting a puppy, you may need to enlist the help of family, friends, or Doggie Daycare to help raise the pup.

If your dog is only digging in one location, you can discourage it. Make a ball of chicken wire and bury it in the hole. As the dog tries to dig again, his toenails will get caught on the wire and he will probably decide to stop the digging. If the dog just digs up the ball of wire, your ball is too small! Try something the size of a basketball. Sometimes you can discourage digging by filling the holes with dog poop. If your dog is at all fastidious, when he discovers the excrement in the hole, he might take up a new hobby!

CHAPTER 22

HOUSEHOLD DESTRUCTION

Dogs destroy things in the house for different reasons. Sometimes it's prompted by anxiety and often it's just boredom. "Separation Anxiety" is a term used to describe a dog that panics when it is away from the owner or other dogs. Many dogs experience stress and panic when there are gunshots or thunderstorms causing loud noises. In a state of panic, dogs look for places to hide, which can cause scratching and biting damage to doors, walls, dog beds, furniture, etc. I once had a dog so upset by thunderstorms that he tried to eat his way into the refrigerator door seeking a place to hide!

A dog is never spiteful. Since dogs only live in the present, it is not possible for a dog to plan to destroy something because of something that happened to him in the past. The damage is simply a response to a panicked state of mind and a "flight response" to escape.

Damage also occurs when dogs are left unattended for long periods of time. Remembering dogs never get any older mentally than a two-year-old child, it's not difficult to imagine what might happen if a two-year-old was left unsupervised in the house for hours. "Home Alone!"

With careful management and maturity, older dogs and dogs that are confident in their surroundings, can be left free in a home safely. Puppies, recently adopted dogs, and sound sensitive or thunder phobic dogs may never earn this freedom.

What is your dog supposed to do in the house in your absence? Dogs are not able to watch television. They can't make phone calls, invite friends over, or use the computer. So, what should your dog do for long periods of time alone in the house? Chewing a bone and playing with toys will only last for a brief period of time.

Ideally, your dog should sleep and rest when you are away. To teach him to do this, confine him in a small, safe space like a dog crate or pen. Once you teach a dog to sleep in a crate, which the dog views as his den, you can get him in the habit of sleeping when you need to leave. "Crate Training" is started with puppies or any dog that needs to learn to be alone. The crate should be introduced for short periods of time at first. Always feed the dog in his crate so it becomes a place he will want to go. Review the SECTION TWO on Housebreaking in this book for more information about crate training, uses of crates, and where to purchase a crate.

CHAPTER 23

COMING WHEN CALLED

Teaching a dog to come to you when you call him is the most important thing he ever learns. If you know your dog will always come when called, he will be there to teach everything else!

The reality is, most dogs *will* come if they have nothing better to do. This does not mean they understand the meaning of the word used or under what conditions they must respond.

Dogs are not born understanding the meaning of "Come." While it is true that up until 16 weeks of age, most puppies tend to stay close to home and their "pack," this does not continue unless the dog is educated. (Review "Understanding Puppyhood" in SECTION ONE of this book.)

Choose one word (any verbal language) to teach a dog to "Come." Do *not* include the dog's name in the teaching of this word. (Review the section on "Speaking Dog" in SECTION ONE of this book to understand why not to use the dog's name.) Be consistent and only use the chosen recall word to call the dog. "Come-on," "Come-ere," "Come over here," are not the same as "Come." Everyone in the household must use the same command. Since voices vary, and dogs don't spell, the dog needs to become familiar with how each family member's recall command sounds. This requires time and practice.

It's always easier to teach a word if the dog has no previous association with it. If you have spent weeks yelling "Come" and allowing the dog to ignore you, now that you want to begin teaching recall, choose a different command word. The dog already knows that the "Come" command will not be enforced. "Here" is often a good choice.

Always teach a dog or puppy a "Come" command by first putting him on a leash. This way you can be assured that you can show the pup how to respond correctly in the learning stages. Attach the leash to a wide buckle or Martingale collar so as not to damage the dog's neck. When the dog/puppy is on a 6-foot leash, show the pup a treat and lure (have him follow food) the dog to you. Decide where you want your dog to end up following the recall. Do you want the dog sitting in front of you or at your side? Either side? Whichever side is closest? The dog's destination near you is very important because dogs think in terms of site pictures. (Review "How Dogs Think" in SECTION ONE of this book.) The dog will eventually associate the command with the picture of where he will end up near you. Humans think of recall in terms of traveling to a person. Dogs more likely think about the picture of where they end up.

As the dog comes to you following the food (luring) and gets to the recall location, give your recall command. After a few repetitions, the dog will start to anticipate the word "Come" means a treat will move and when he follows the food and arrives at a specific destination, he will get to eat it.

Whenever you use treats to teach a dog something, make sure the dog is hungry and has not recently finished a meal. We use treats to teach new concepts but once the dog shows understanding, the treats are removed. You can fade using treats by using them intermittently and by using a "pretend" or "air-cookie" so the dog thinks you have the treat at first but then realizes you don't. Using treats to teach a recall is simple but this is not the end of the process. Make sure to practice the recall in many different locations and around distractions. Increase the distance the dog can get away from you by using a longer leash. All the teaching is initially done on leash to assure the dog actually has no choice, but to come to you. Never repeat commands. This does not instruct a dog to respond to the first command you give.

As you add distractions, the dog may decide he is not really interested in returning to your side. Perhaps the sight of another animal, an interesting smell, or the ability to run is more exciting than the cookie you are offering. This is where the leash gives you the advantage. After giving *one* command to "Come," if the dog, for any reason, does not respond immediately and return to you, give a quick, short jerk on the leash to interrupt whatever the dog is doing. The jerk is a quick snap motion and is not strong enough to move the dog. You are trying to interrupt the dog's distracted thinking, not force him to come. If the dog turns to look at you or starts to come towards you, PRAISE VERBALLY. If not, continue the jerk *and release* of the leash until the dog decides he would rather come to you for the cookie than stay with the distraction and be repeatedly interrupted. Do not repeat the "Come" command. Repeating commands does not teach and actually causes the dog to ignore you. You will always succeed. Life, as the dog knows it, does not continue until he comes to you! (Review "The Power of Time" in SECTION ONE of this book.)

Many people make the mistake of using the leash improperly. Never pull or reel the dog into you like a big fish. This only teaches the dog he must return if he is on a line. We want the dog to *decide* it is in his best interest to move towards you so that you will stop interrupting him with quick jerks on the line. It must be the dog's decision to come to you so it will eventually be reliable off leash. Jerks on the line should **not** be hard enough to move the dog; just quick pops to interrupt what he is thinking about. Think of the jerk as a snap of a rubber band. It's sudden; not strong.

Work with the dog on a longer and longer leash and in different locations. When the dog is responding immediately to one recall command and you are no longer using a treat, it's time to drop the long line. Go to a safe, fenced space with the dog on a 35 to 50 foot line. (If your dog is large and fast, use a longer line.) Walk around and let the dog drag the line.

When the dog gets distracted by a sight or smell, call the dog once. If the dog responds, praise immediately. If the dog does not respond, pick up the end of the long line and jerk and release it until the dog either looks at you or makes the decision to return to you. When the dog looks at you or starts to move in your direction, praise verbally. On average, it will take 35 different locations for the dog to generalize that he must come when called, under all conditions.

When dragging the long leash, if the dog comes to you without you calling it, praise the behavior anyway. Anticipation is the first step of learning, so this is common.

After teaching the recall on the long leash, without treats, and in many different locations, if you have not had to pick up the line and jerk it for multiple sessions, you may be ready to begin off leash training. If it does not go well, you can always put the line back on the dog. Off leash freedom is a privilege for dogs and this privilege can be lost at any time if the dog forgets his lessons.

Begin off leash recall training in a small, safe space. A small outdoor yard or indoor room works well. Wait for the dog to become distracted by something and give the recall command one time. If the dog responds immediately, praise verbally. If the dog, realizing he is off a line, does not respond, slowly walk towards him, take hold of his collar and bring him to you. Think of your hand and arm as being a leash. When the dog gets to the appropriate location by your side or in front of you, praise him verbally and release him from the command. Repeat this exercise, always waiting for the dog to get distracted until the dog, knowing you will come get him anyway, decides to come to you after one recall command.

If the dog chooses to run away from you as you walk towards him, throw something suddenly on the ground near the dog. A piece of a small chain, keys, metal food bowl, shoe, or shaker bottle will work. This act of throwing something on the floor will interrupt the running away long enough for you to call him again (yes you can repeat the command once following a thrown object) and see if he has changed his mind. If the dog continues to try to run from you, continue to throw things. All dogs will give up and either come to you or allow you to get them and bring them to you. Usually, dogs are very wary to try running away again since this solution to their problem didn't work very well. Do not try to scare the dog. Smaller dogs need smaller, softer objects thrown. You might use a bean bag for a small dog.

For very sensitive dogs, try throwing a soft toy near them. Even if the dog picks up the toy, the unexpected toss will interrupt his unwanted behavior. Your goal is to convince the dog things will fly through the air and land near him if he does not come immediately when you call him.

Throwing things near a dog that is running away and offering him another option to come to you for praise, helps the dog make a better decision. If it seems harsh to you, remember that ending up under the wheels of a car for not responding to a recall command is much worse.

Many dogs never need anything thrown at them. They learn from the long line to come to you and realize you will move to get them if they don't. Only the more independent dogs and dogs that have been running away for a long time, will need to get to the level of flying objects to convince them you have magic powers and can reach them through the air.

CHAPTER 24

TEACHING STAY

"Stay" means remain in position and do not move your body as I leave you. Following a "Stay" command, the owner either releases the dog from a distance away or returns to the dog's side and then releases him. If you tell a dog to sit and have no intention of leaving him, the dog should remain in the sitting position until released and there is no need for a "stay" command. Since "stay" means do not move your body when I leave you, an owner should never tell a dog to "stay" and then walk through a door and leave for work. While the behavior of not bolting through doors can be taught, it is not a "stay." All commands must have a clear meaning to both the owner and the dog. (Review CONSISTENCY in SECTION ONE of this book.)

When teaching a dog to remain in position, I never use food. Food is a motivator, and we don't want the dog thinking about moving to get to food. Besides, the best reward for staying is the freedom to move!

"Stay" can be taught to most dogs that are five months old or older. Puppies younger than this are too busy and not mentally capable of holding a thought for an extended period of time. Male dogs and puppies that will become large dogs should start learning to stay a little older as they mature more slowly.

To teach "Stay," begin with a dog on a leash and a Martingale collar. Tell the dog to sit as this is the easiest position to learn to stay in. Command "Stay" one time and simultaneously place the palm of your hand closest to the dog, in front of his eyes. Next, move directly in front of the dog as you put your hand back to your side. Wait until the dog gets up. When the dog moves out of the sit-stay, gently reposition him using the collar and leash. As soon as the dog is returned to the sitting position, praise verbally. It is not necessary to repeat the command since the dog does not understand it anyway! The dog should understand your verbal praise for returning to the sitting position. If the dog gets up again, respond the same way by gently repositioning the dog and praising him. If the dog remains in position for 10 to 15 seconds, return to the dog and verbally release him.

Gradually add distance between you and the dog. Always make sure that the dog makes at least one mistake that you fix, before releasing him. The only way a dog learns what "stay" means is to get up and find out what happens. If you are having difficulty getting the dog to make a mistake, try harder. Try stepping to one side or the other, bowing to the dog, dropping a toy or food etc. There are always ways to present the dog with a new site picture and cause a mistake. Dogs learn through trial and error. You must cause the errors for learning to occur. Once you master a stay in the sitting position, you can do the same in the down position. Increase distance, duration, distractions, and add multiple locations before you progress to off leash training.

Why does the dog learn to stay in a sitting position with this technique? Every time the dog gets up, he is repositioned and praised. If he gets up 25 times, you replace and praise him 25 times. (No extra commands!) The dog soon realizes it's easier to just sit there than to make the effort to get up. The dog decides it is to *his advantage* to remain where you left him until you release him, because it takes less effort. You have gotten your dog to make a better decision without any harshness or food!

CHAPTER 25

WORKING WITH SHY DOGS

When a dog is untrusting of humans or wants to hide or run away, it is especially important to understand how to communicate clearly. The principles of how a dog learns and how they think applies to shy dogs as well as confident ones.

Remember everything you allow a dog to do, the dog thinks you approve of. If you permit a shy dog to hide behind your legs, you are telling the dog this behavior is acceptable. Even when a dog is fearful, sometimes the only way to deal with fear is to face it. Holding a dog on a Martingale collar and leash and preventing it from hiding behind you as you praise verbally will quickly explain to the dog hiding is not the best solution to solve his problem. Growling because a dog is afraid when a person or other dog approaches is not acceptable behavior. The person at the end of the leash should interrupt the growling with a tug on the leash, touch on the head, or the sound of a shaker bottle and verbally praise immediately. It will take some repetition, but the dog will decide growling is not producing a desired result.

Shy dogs do not need to be touched by strangers. Prevent people from reaching for them or staring at them as this is viewed by the dog as a threat. Have a stranger stand about two feet away making no eye contact. Instruct the stranger to lower their arm and hand against their body. If the dog chooses to sniff or move towards the person, praise verbally. If the dog holds its ground and does not growl, praise the dog and have the stranger back away. From experience, nervous dogs have learned if they growl, people will back away. They use this technique to maintain their "personal space." When we insist through interruption and praise that growling is not acceptable, we must also allow the dog to see the person retreat without being growled at.

People mistakenly think if a stranger offers the shy dog a cookie, the dog will be friendly. This rarely works. Shy dogs are often leery of strangers offering treats as this has been used to catch or trap them in the past. Besides, why do you want to teach your dog to take food from a stranger? Is this really a good lesson? Most shy dogs are so stressed they will not even eat food when near strangers. If your dog or puppy eats food when stressed, the *owner* can hold a treat for the pup near the leg of the stranger and encourage the dog to take it. This is the best way to use food correctly to explain to the dog you believe this person is safe. The dog's confidence comes from the owner who the dog has trust in.

Shy and nervous dogs benefit from education. Anything you teach a hesitant dog helps to make them more confident. Sometimes just learning they can step over something or climb onto something gives them a sense of accomplishment. The more a dog understands how to learn and communicate with its owner, the calmer and more secure they become. It really doesn't matter what you teach a dog but teach them things. Whether it's tricks, agility, tracking, herding, obedience, frisbee, or swimming; everything the dog learns helps build his self-esteem.

Dogs are very resilient. Anything bad a dog has learned, he can relearn correctly. It is also true; anything a dog learns, he will know forever. People forget, but dogs remember everything that happens to them and everything they learn. I have taken dogs that have been retired from competition for years and when asked to perform what they used to do in a trial, they do it like the day they retired. If you think your dog has forgotten how to do something, I suggest he never really learned it. Remember, dogs often do things correctly, long before they understand what they are doing and under what conditions they must do it. People mistakenly jump to the conclusion that because a dog responds correctly, he knows what he is doing. This is not true. Until the dog performs correctly in many different environments and amidst many different distractions, you should not assume understanding.

CHAPTER 26

UNDERSTANDING RESOURCE GUARDING

Resource guarding is a term dog trainers/behaviorists use to describe a dog that becomes aggressive when it thinks something that belongs to them is being threatened. Resource guarding is a normal dog behavior but like most things, too much of a "good thing" is no good!

Dogs are inclined to guard food bowls, toys, bones, stolen items (socks, paper items, gloves, etc.) other dogs, and even people. Basically, anything they deem valuable can result in guarding behavior. This behavior can begin as a puppy but often does not rear its ugly head until the dog becomes a young adult. Some dogs guard only food or a toy, others guard multiple items.

Guarding often begins with a growl, lip curl, stiffening of body, crouched position and may progress to lunging, baring teeth, and barking. All breeds of dogs are capable of these actions, but some breeds are more prone to it. For example, female German Shepherds are frequently overly possessive of their owners. While some owners like to feel guarded by their dogs, be careful, because the dog will also guard you from your friends and family. This is not a behavior that should ever be permitted in a domestic setting.

Dogs/puppies raised with limited access to food, in crowded conditions, with multiple size dogs around, may learn to guard as self-preservation. It is not uncommon to find this behavior in dogs rescued from puppy mills or hoarding situations. This is not always the case. Truth be told, I have known dogs with no reason to guard, who grow up with this tendency. Because of these observations, I believe some resource guarding behavior is learned, and some is genetic.

Anything a dog learns can be unlearned. Genetic personality disorders are usually not extinguished through training and rely more on management of environment than trying to change behavior.

It never hurts to attempt to re-educate a pup, but when behaviors do not improve, management is the best option. It's always easier if the dog guards only one item. Keep this in mind as you decide whether to work to change a dog's behavior or manage the environment to avoid triggering resource guarding.

If your dog resource guards his food bowl, put the bowl in your lap as you sit in a chair. Feed the dog in small amounts from your hand. Continue feeding this way for a few weeks. Next progress to putting a small amount of food in the bowl and holding the bowl for the dog to eat out of. Gradually increase the amount of food you put in the bowl until the dog's entire meal is being eaten out of the bowl you are holding. At any time the dog stiffens, growls, or shows any aggression, remove the food and bowl, and go about your business. Try again a few hours later. When the dog realizes the guarding behavior causes the food, bowl, and you to disappear, he may decide to change his behavior.

If you are sitting on the couch with a dog next to you and another dog or person approaches, this might prompt guarding behavior. If the dog next to you growls or demonstrates any aggression, get up and leave the room without the dog. Hopefully, the guarding dog will make the association that guarding behavior causes the resource being guarded to disappear and is therefore not to his advantage.

There is no "correction" that will stop resource guarding. If a dog exhibits resource guarding behavior, the best you can do is try to interrupt the behavior with a sound (rattle bottle, metal chain, air horn) or touch (throw something that lands near the dog to break the dog's focus on guarding) and immediately praise and remove the object being guarded. Any attempt to correct a dog for growling makes things worse. The growl is a warning signal and important canine communication. We never want to discourage this warning because it may prompt the dog to lash out without warning!

For dogs genetically predisposed to resource guarding, management is often the best approach. Avoid triggers (food and toys) when around other dogs or people. Feed dogs separately and do not give treats in a group. Leave a leash on a dog so you can easily remove the dog from a situation that might lead to guarding.

Resource guarding may not be fixable when it is a personality quirk. The worst part of it is we may not know a dog has this tendency until it is older. Rescuing older dogs has the advantage of knowing the personality a dog has developed. People often prefer to get a puppy because they feel they can mold a puppy into anything they want. This is not reality.

CHAPTER 27

INTRODUCING NEW DOGS

Anytime we introduce a new dog into a household of other dogs, we need to be aware of dog behavior. Whether the new dog is visiting for a day, staying permanently, or being temporarily fostered, bringing a new dog into a household can be tricky.

Always make introductions outside of the house. When dogs meet in open space and away from "their territory" there is less tension. Introduce dogs on a leash or with a chain link fence between them or both.

The natural progression of greeting for dogs is a lot of sniffing, diverting of eyes, and lots of movement of tails, ears and bodies. If a dog stiffens or stares, it is a warning that the dog is challenging the other dog and should be immediately separated or interrupted. If a dog puts his head or front legs over the back or neck of the other dog, it's a sign this dog wants to dominate the other dog. If the other dog is submissive and rolls onto his back, this will resolve itself. If both dogs are dominant, the dog being mounted will object and this can cause a fight. Again, interrupt the behavior.

Once dogs seem comfortable being around each other and their body language is friendly (everyone is moving freely), you can remove leashes in a small space. It never hurts to have a shaker bottle (bottle with rocks or pennies in it) in case there is behavior you need to interrupt.

If all goes well, repeat the on-leash introduction in the house. This should not take as much time as the dogs are already familiar with the smells of each other.

Just like humans, some dogs like each other immediately, some take time to warm up, and some will never get along. In a multiple dog household, it's important you add a dog that will fit into your pack. With a small group, it's easier with an even number of dogs. Having three dogs presents an "odd man out" scenario unless one of the dogs is much older and then it will work. One male and one female is usually an easy combination. Keeping a pack of all females or all males works too. I currently live with twelve bitches. They all get along as long as I'm careful who I add. If I bring one male dog into the pack, the girls will fight with each other over the male, even if he is neutered! Multiple dog households with dogs and bitches in numbers is often a problem as fights will occur as the dogs compete for attention, food, or each other.

Sometimes dogs get along for many months and then after one fight, they are incompatible. It's as if they can't forget the argument even when they don't remember what the fight was about. When this happens, it is usually only resolved by separating the dogs.

Certain breeds are easier in groups. Sporting dogs, herding dogs, and hounds tend to be more gregarious and easy going, while terriers and dogs bred to guard can be more selective. Each dog has its own unique personality. Different breeds of dogs communicate and play differently. For example, Labradors and Australian Shepherds think nothing of body slamming each other in play. Boxers like to swat and play with their paws. Poodles do a lot of play bowing and leaping in the air. Terriers like to be vocal and play-fight. Border Collies choose to run around other dogs and herd them. When you have multiple dogs of the same breed, they communicate well but when you mix breeds, the dogs don't always like the type of play being offered. This can cause altercations.

Most dogs are very tolerant of adding puppies of any breed to a pack. Problems start as the puppy becomes an adult and may start to challenge the other dogs to find his place in the pack.

Neutering males and spaying female dogs helps reduce the tension in multi dog homes but it is no guarantee of compatibility.

CHAPTER 28

DOGS ARE MY TEACHERS

Over the last 50+ years of living with multiple dogs and training thousands, dogs have taught me most of what you read in this book. Studying dog behavior and learning to communicate in the language of "Dog" has been a major focus in my life. I write this book so others can learn from what the dogs have taught me.

The longer I work with dogs, the less I say to them and the faster they learn. It is not necessary to ever verbally tell a dog when they are wrong. They know from your physical reaction or non-reaction something is not as it should be. Have you ever played the game of "charades?" It's a parlor game in which words or phrases are represented in pantomime. Communicating in the language of "Dog" is a lot like Charades because dogs understand motion, not words.

I never use the word "No." It is not helpful to tell dogs what **not** to do. Remember, it's like sending you to the store with a shopping list of everything you should not buy! How long will it take you to shop? If you don't need spaghetti sauce, why even think about it?

If you don't want a dog to do something, why draw his attention to the thing you don't want? It works against you. People are forever telling dogs, "No bark, no bite, don't eat that, don't get on the couch, don't jump" and think that this somehow instructs the dog how to behave. The dog doesn't have a clue what behavior is appropriate. Focus on the behaviors you want and interrupt the unwanted ones.

When you stop issuing so many commands and spend more time "listening" (by observing a dog's actions) to what the dog is saying, communication grows. When you give dogs time to think, they do.

Every dog trainer is the product of the dogs they have trained. Each dog I have spent time with has taught me something. If a trainer works with only large dogs or small dogs, or sporting dogs or working/guard dogs, their perspective on how dogs learn is different from trainers who have learned to speak "Dog" in many different dialects over the years. Trainers who claim you can train all dogs with only treats, have not met the independent, strong-willed dogs I have, or perhaps they have not needed to train them to high levels of performance. Those who have only worked with large, strong, independent dogs cannot appreciate how gently you can modify behavior on some sensitive dogs. There is no good way to really learn about dogs without allowing the dogs themselves to teach you.

I wish I had a dollar for every client who came to the realization halfway through their first lesson that it was them, and not the dog, who needed to learn the most! Then there are the humans who believe their dog is stupid or just "doesn't listen" realizing after a few minutes of a lesson, that their dogs are brilliant but do not speak English. Communicating with a dog in their own language produces instant results and happy pups and owners.

Changing dog behavior is easy. Dogs are predictable. They never get any older than a two-year-old child. Unlike a child, dogs don't lie. They will always do whatever they believe is to their advantage to do. Dogs are very forgiving and resilient. People are much more complicated!

I hope I have given you some different ways of understanding dog behavior. Getting dogs to make better decisions is a lot more fun than trying to force or bribe a dog. Building a working relationship with your dog based on trust, fairness, and respect offers a level of communication that any dog and owner will value.